2ND EDITION
BIG TV WORKBOOK

1

Pearson Education Limited
KAO Two
KAO Park
Harlow
Essex CM17 9NA
England
and Associated Companies throughout the world.

www.English.com/BigEnglish2

© Pearson Education Limited 2017

First published 2017

ISBN: 978-1-292-20358-4

Set in Heinemann Roman

Printed in Italy by L.E.G.O. S.p.A.

Acknowledgements

The publisher would like to thank the following for their kind permission to reproduce their photographs:

(Key: b-bottom; c-centre; l-left; r-right; t-top)

123RF.com: 3quarks 32c/8, 4cl/4, 4b (b), 7c (bike), 7cr (train), 7r (boy), 11cr, 12tl/2, 12cr/7, 15b, 19br, 20tr/4, 21t, 23br, 27cr, 27br (boy), 31br, 35cr, 36t/1, 36t/3, 39cr, 4cl/4, 4b (b), 7c (bike), 7cr (train), 7r (boy), 11cr, 12tl/2, 12cr/7, 15b, 19br, 20tr/4, 21t, 23br, 27cr, 27br (boy), 31br, 35cr, 36t/1, 36t/3, 39cr, 4cl/4, 4b (b), 7c (bike), 7cr (train), 7r (boy), 11cr, 12tl/2, 12cr/7, 15b, 19br, 20tr/4, 21t, 23br, 27cr, 27br (boy), 31br, 35cr, 36t/1, 36t/3, 39cr, Agnieszka Murphy 4bc (b), albertus engbers 32t/l, Aleksandra Abu Haltam 9bl, 33br, Alexandra Yurkina 31cl, Alexey Zaitsev 29t/b, alexutemov 35cr (umbrella), andegro4ka 19tr, 28b/b, Andrei Nekrassov 20br, Andrei Tronin 9tl, Andriy Popov 4b (a), ankomando 9b, Anna Bogatyreva 27tl, Anton Starikov 10c, Antonio Balaguer Soler 21br, Armen Bogush 37tl, bbtreesubmission 27br (lion), Benoit Chartron 6cl, Bernard Rabone 22cl, bloodua 5b, 29br, blueringmedia 10cl, 10br, 23cr, 28b/c, 30br, 39tl, 39tl (ted), 39tc (scott), 39tr, Brankica Valaskovic 30cr, Brian Scantlebury 21tc, Chermen Otaraev, Cindy Eccles 32t/3, coliap 6cr, 6br, comodo777 6bc, Daniel Thornberg, devnenski 4c/5, Dmitriy Baranov 32c/5, dmstudio 28br/c, 30bc, 31cl (chocolate), dolgachov 37bl, domenicogelermo 12cl/6, Duncan Cook Drummond 20tc/3, dzein (blue), 35c (red), Elena Schweitzer 28tr/4, epicstockmedia 32c/6, Evgenii Naumov 17br, felisredcat 6bl, frinz 33tr, gbh007 36t/4, gelpi 11cl, 19bl, 23b, 27bl, 31bl, 35cl, Goodluz, Graham Oliver 25bl, graphicbee 13t, 15cr, happymay 18cl, heinteh 28cl/5, iamnee 31cr (mooncakes), Igor terekhov 16bc/b, Igor Zakowski 27t, iimages 22c, 22bc, 27tl (rabbit), 27tr (horse), 39t, Ijupco, ika747 10cr, IKO, Ioulia Bolchakova 13tl, Ivan Ryabokon 18bc, Izflzf 37tr, Jennifer Huls 13bl, jiaking1 28bc/b, Jozef Polc 16b/b, jvdwolf, kakigori 9tr, 11b, 11bc, 11br, 23t, 23tr, kankhem 35, Kanstantsin Prymachuk 16tl/1, Klara Viskova 26bl (lamb), 27l (tiger), ladyann 23cl, LI TZU CHEIN 38c, 38cl, 38cr, 38bl, 38bc, 38br, Liubou Yasiukovich 8c, Luc De Salterain 31cr (pink cake), magone, mallinka 4bl (a), Marco Antonio Hayashi Palazuelos 10bc, margouillat 28tl/2, Maryna Mykhalskq 31c, Massimo Greggio 32br, Maxim Popov 15tc, 22cr, 23c, 30c, maxst 12cl/5, maxym 4tl/l, michaeljung 28tl/2, mohamad hafiz ma'ail 32t/4, moremarinka, Muhammad Desta Laksana 27tr, nad1992 5t (b), Narintorn Pornsuknimitkul 33tc, Nikita Chisnikov 28bl/a, Oleksandr Dorokhov 18c, Oleksiy Kovalenko 18bl, Olena Bolotova 15cl, Olga Sokolva 10bl, pahham 12bc, petkov 21tr, petovarga 7br, Petr Student 4br (c), photoroad 33tl, Pieter ten Broek 34b, pongsak kaewmanaprasert 28tc/3, poonotsuke 5tr (d), pratyaksa 13tr, prudencio alvarez 37tc, prykhodov 12br, reginast777 37b, Robertas Pezas 19cr, robuart 19cl, rocsprod 4cr/6, rosipro 8cl/5, Sandra van der steen 36c/8, sararoom 18cr, sarininka 28b/a, sbworld8 12tr/4, seamartini 30bl, Sofia Vlasiuk, stable 32t/2, steinar14 22bl, stockbroker 8cl/6, 8cr/8, stockshoppe 5bl, 15tl, stylephotographs 36c/5, sudowoodo 9tc, svelby 25b, Tatyana Okhitina 31cr (gingerbread man), Teguh Mujiono 7t, 19t, 26cl, 26bl, 27tl (lamb), 27r (lamb), 27r (lion), 27br, 35t, tele52 23r, tomaccojc 7bc (c), undrey 30cl, Viktorija Reuta 19tc, Vladimir Vancik 13tc, Vladimir Yudin 4b (c), 5tc (c), Volha Shaukavets 29/c, wang Tom 12b, 32bl, Wavebreak Media Ltd. 8tc/3, Xiaojiao Wang, Yelena Panyukova 22br, Yevgeniy IIyin 6c, Yevhenly Dorofyeyev 18br, yobro 10 8b, yulia87 29t/a, yupiramos 13b, 35cr (multi), yuyuyi 11bl, zefart, zzizar 26cr; **Pearson Education Ltd:** 36c/6, Malcolm Harris, Pearson Education, Inc. 35br, Amit John 26bc, Pearson Education Australia Pty Ltd 25tr, Ratan Mani Banerjee. Pearson India Education Services Pvt. Ltd 21b, 26c, 29b, Jules Selmes 12tl/1, 12tr/3, Martin Sookias 4tr/3; **Shutterstock.com:** 2016443 20c/6, 2117717 7cl (taxi), aastock 7l, 15bl, 15br, Africa Studio 16tc/3, alexandre zveiger 20cl/5, Alexey Nikolaew 16bc/c, Andreas Gradin, Andrey Yurlov 17tl, Aneese 24tl/4, Atetia, Atthapol Saita, B-A-C-O 7b, BrianWancho 12cr/8, Coprid 16b/a (red cap), CREATISTA 8c/7, Daria Rybakova 24tr/5, 24br, dotstock 17t, Eric Isselee 24tl/2, 24tr/4, 24cr/9, @erics, Erik Lam 24cl/7, 24cr/8, Ewelina Wachala 20tl/1, 20bc, Gemenacom 16c/6, George Rudy 36c/7, Gilles Lougassi 21tl, Goodluz 4tc/2, Graeme Shannon 10tr, Gwoeii 16cl/4, homydesign 16br/c, iymsts 16cl/5, Jacek Chabraszewski 7r, JIANG HONGYAN 28tc/6, John Abbate 16b/a (hat), Jose Ignacio Soto 25tc, Julian Rovagnati 17b, K.Miri Photography 16tl/2, 16br/b, KAMONRAT 24cl/6, 24bc, Karkas 16tr/7, Klara Viskova 33b, kuroksta 5tl (a), Lilu330 15tr, Liveshot 16b/a, Ljupco Smokovski 36t/2, m.bonotto 32bc, Matthew Cole 36br, MaxyM 25tl, Mikhail Pogosov 17c, Monkey Business Images 17tr, nattanan726 8tl/2, Olga Popova 16bl/c, ollyy 20tl/2, Phoenixns 14b, Regein Paassen 7cr, Ruth Black 28cr/7, Sergey Novikov 32c/7, Sergio33 28tl/l, stockfotoart 20bl, szafei 8tr/4, urfin 24tc/3, 24bl, V.Belov 20cr/7, Victor Brave 31tl, 31tr, Vitalinka 8tl/l, Volodymyr Burdiak, Voronin76 12bl, Wire_man 7bl

Stickers

123RF.com: Daniel Thornberg, Duncan Cook, gbh007, Goodluz, juvwolf, maxym, rocsprod, V.Xiaojiano, Xiaojiao Wang, zefart;
Shutterstock.com: George, V.Belov

All other images © Pearson Education

Every effort has been made to trace the copyright holders and we apologise in advance for any unintentional omissions. We would be pleased to insert the appropriate acknowledgement in any subsequent edition of this publication.

Contents

1 School Time

I **will learn about** traveling to school.

🎧2 1 Listen, look, and say.

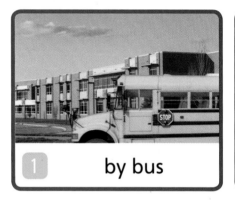

1 by bus

2 on foot

3 by train

4 by car

5 by bicycle

6 by taxi

🎧3 2 Listen and check (✓).

a

b

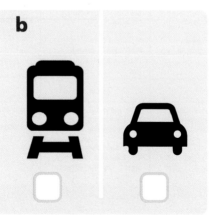

c

3 Read, count and circle.

a I see **two / three** cars.

b I see **two / four** bicycles.

c I see **one / two** bus.

d I see **three / four** taxis.

4 How do you go to school? Ask and answer with a partner. Draw.

5 ▶ⓥ **Watch and stick in order. Then say.**

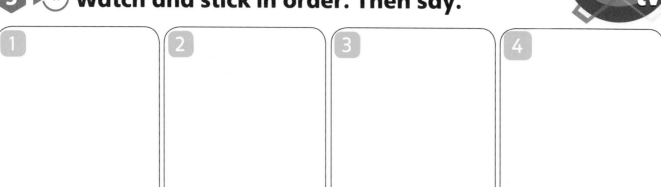

| 1 | 2 | 3 | 4 |

6 ▶ⓥ **Watch again. Match.**

a Miles   USA   by taxi

b Amanda   UK   home school

7 🎧 **Listen, read, and check (✓).**

a In Indonesia, the children have to cross …

b They must carry their …

c At school, let's hope their feet are …

8 **Follow the maze. Say with a partner.**

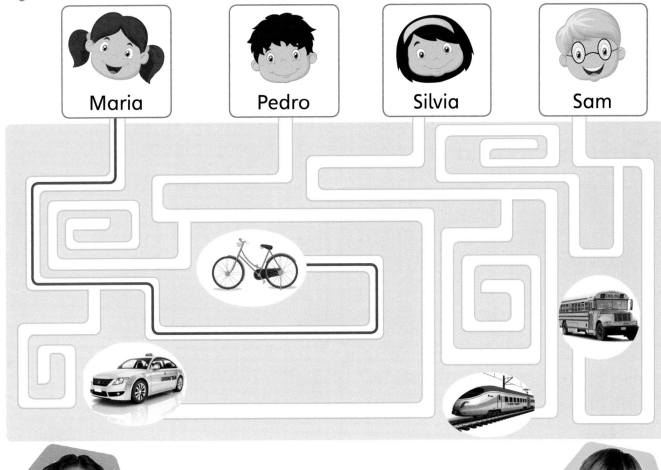

Maria   Pedro   Silvia   Sam

Maria goes to school …

… by bicycle!

9 **Look and write.**

a It's a **car**.   **b** It's a _____.   **c** They're _____.   **d** They're _____.

THINK BIG

How do children around the world go to school?

2 A New Family

I will learn about families.

5

1 Listen, look, and say.

1 family

2 baby

3 mother

4 father

5 sister

6 brother

7 cousins

8 friends

2 Look, read and match.

a brother

c father

b mother

d baby

3 **Read and write for you.**

a How many brothers do you have? _____

b How many cousins do you have? _____

c How many friends do you have? _____

4 **How many family members do you have? Ask and answer with a partner. Draw your family.**

5 ▶(v2) **Watch. Check (✓) what you hear or see.**

☐ baby ☐ mother ☐ father ☐ sister

6 ▶(v2) **Watch again. Write Yes or No.**

a Is Ndotto from Kenya? _____

b Is Ndotto two years old? _____

c Does Ndotto like milk? _____

7 **Read and circle.**

a Ndotto has no **mother** / **friend**.

b The elephant wants to be Ndotto's big **sister** / **mother**.

c Now Ndotto has a big elephant **family** / **cousin**.

8 **Listen, read, and check (✓).**

a As a baby, Ndotto lives with …

b They feed him …

c Ndotto likes playing with …

☐

☐

☐

☐

☐

☐

9 **Find and circle the words.**

j	x	c	o	u	s	i	n
h	s	i	s	t	e	r	f
f	a	m	i	l	y	w	a
p	n	e	a	h	e	l	t
e	j	b	a	b	y	y	h
f	r	i	e	n	d	g	e
j	i	m	o	t	h	e	r
w	b	r	o	t	h	e	r

Word list

baby

brother

cousin

~~family~~

father

friend

mother

sister

10 **Match. Then ask and answer with a partner.**

a I have three brothers.
b I have three sisters.
c I have one brother.
d I have two brothers and one sister.

a

How many brothers and sisters do you have?

I have one brother and two sisters.

THINK BIG Where are the biggest families in the world?
Where are the smallest?

Use Your Body

I will learn about body actions.

7

1 Listen, look, and say.

1 touch

2 see

3 smell

4 taste

5 hear

6 play

7 speak

8 sign

2 Match.

a hear　　b play　　c sign　　d speak

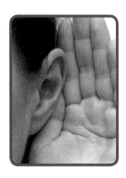

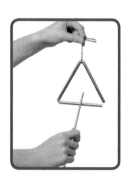

3 **Look, read and match.**

   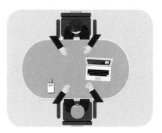

a He touches the window. **b** He plays the piano. **c** They touch the table. **d** She plays the drums.

4 **What are the five senses? Ask and answer with a partner. Draw.**

5 ▶(V3) **Watch and stick in order. Then say.**

1	2	3	4

6 ▶(V3) **Watch again. Match.**

a | Children in Sao Paulo | | play a window

b | Curtis | | sign

c | Bruno | | play the piano

7 ◖)) **Read and circle. Then listen and check.**

a We use our **bodies** / **heads** to communicate with the world.

b We need our hands and our feet to **touch** / **play** the drums.

c Some children in Sao Paulo use their hands to **hear** / **speak**.

8 **Look. Ask and answer with a partner.**

Gary

Harry   Mandy

Bob

Jan   John

Stella

Does Gary play the drums?

No, he doesn't. He plays the piano.

9 **Write. Then listen and say.**

ears   mouth   noses   hands   ~~mouth~~

a I speak with my **mouth**.

b They smell with their _____.

c We sign with our _____.

d She hears with her _____.

e He tastes with his _____.

THINK BIG

Do you play an instrument or a sport? How do you use your body? What do you like to do?

4 Clothes

I will learn about clothes and sports events

1 Listen, look, and say.

1 kit

2 tracksuit

3 scarf

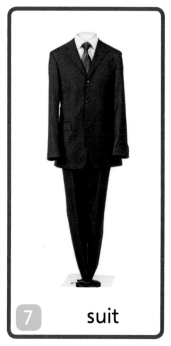

4 hat

5 cap

6 T-shirt

7 suit

2 Listen and circle.

a

b

c

3 Listen, look, and say.

soccer player   team manager   horse race   spectators

4 What clothes do you wear for sports? Ask and answer with a partner. Draw.

5 ▶ᵥ₄ **Watch. Check (✓) what you hear or see.**

⬜ kit   ⬜ tracksuit   ⬜ T-shirt   ⬜ hat

6 ▶ᵥ₄ **Watch again. Match.**

a soccer game   **b** horse race

| kit | top hat | tracksuit | scarf | smart clothes |

7 13 🎧 **Listen, read, and check (✓).**

a Soccer players wear a soccer **kit / tracksuit** for a match.

b Soccer team managers wear a **suit / scarf**.

c Spectators wear their team's colors on **hats / T-shirts**.

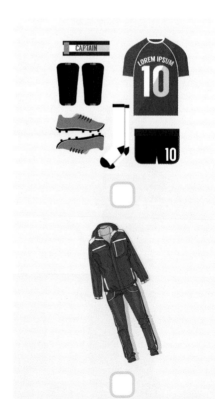

8 **Follow the lines. Ask and answer with a partner.**

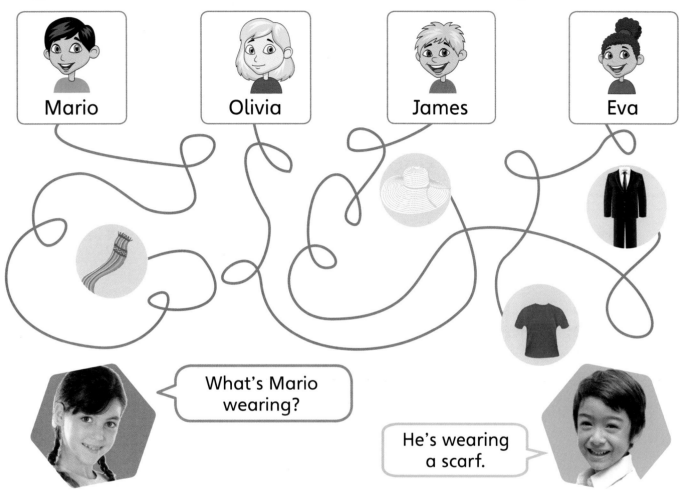

Mario   Olivia   James   Eva

What's Mario wearing?

He's wearing a scarf.

9 **Write the words in order. Listen and check.**

a wearing – green – a – She's – scarf.
She's wearing a green scarf.

b a – He's – hat – red – wearing.

_____

c tracksuit – wearing – I'm – blue – a.

_____

d black – soccer – You're – a – wearing – kit.

_____

What's popular to wear in your country?

5 World Homes

I will learn about different homes.

 1 Listen, look, and say.

1 house	2 student home
3 narrow boat	4 tent

  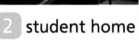  

5 apartment **6** yurt **7** chum

2 Listen and match.

a Sam   **b** Sally   **c** Tom

Stickers

Stickers

9 **Let's Get Active** page 38

3 **Look, read and match.**

a These are solar panels.

b This is a canal.

c These are shipping containers.

d This is a truck.

4 **What's your home like? Ask and answer with a partner. Draw.**

5 ▶ V5 **Watch and stick in order. Then say.**

1	2	3	4

6 ▶ V5 **Watch again. Match.**

a London   student home
b Denmark   yurt
c Siberia   chum
d Mongolia   narrow boat

7 🎧 17 **Listen, read, and check (✓).**

a This is my home. It's a narrow boat.
b My home is an apartment.
c I live in a house.

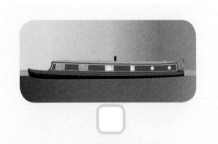
☐

☐

☐

☐

☐

☐

8 **Follow the maze. Ask and answer with a partner.**

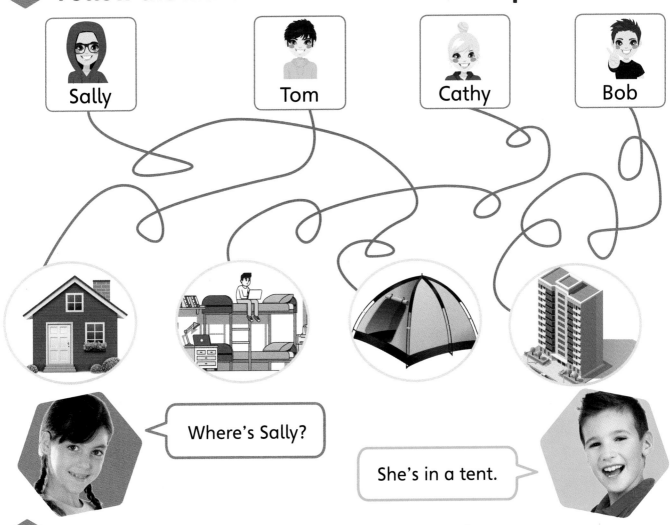

Sally · Tom · Cathy · Bob

Where's Sally?

She's in a tent.

9 **Write the letters in order. Then match.**

a r o w n r a o t a b — A place to live and study.

narrow boat

b n t e t — A home on the water.

_____

c u t e t n s d m e h o — A place to sleep when you go camping.

_____

**Where do your classmates live?
Do a survey and make a chart.**

Interesting Animals

I will learn about different animals.

 1 Listen, look, and say.

 1 guinea pig

 2 rabbit

 3 chicken

 4 sheep

 5 bear

 6 tiger

 7 pony

 8 lamb

 9 lion

2 Look at **1**. Read and write Yes or No.

a Is it a chicken?

b Is it a lamb?

c Is it a bear?

_____

_____

_____

3 Listen, look, and say.

This is a farm.

This is a theme park.

This is an elderly care home.

4 What's your favorite animal?
Ask and answer with a partner. Draw.

BIG tv

5 ▶ⓥ⑥ **Watch. Check (✓) what you hear or see.**

☐ guinea pig ☐ sheep ☐ bear ☐ pony

6 ▶ⓥ⑥ **Watch again. Match.**

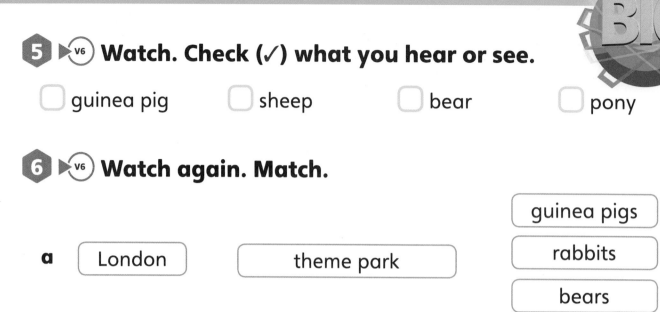

| guinea pigs |
| rabbits |
| bears |
| chickens |
| tigers |
| lions |

a London theme park

b Korea elderly care homes

20
7 🎧 **Listen, read, and check (✓).**

a What is it?
It's a guinea pig.

b What's the sheep doing? It's eating.

c What are the ponies doing? They're running.

8 **Find and circle the words. Ask and answer with a partner.**

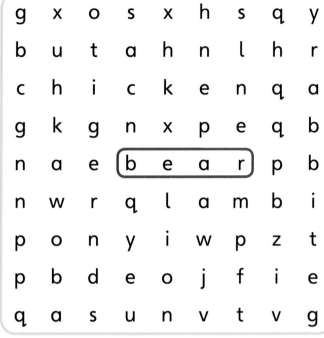

g	x	o	s	x	h	s	q	y
b	u	t	a	h	n	l	h	r
c	h	i	c	k	e	n	q	a
g	k	g	n	x	p	e	q	b
n	a	e	b	e	a	r	p	b
n	w	r	q	l	a	m	b	i
p	o	n	y	i	w	p	z	t
p	b	d	e	o	j	f	i	e
q	a	s	u	n	v	t	v	g

What is it?

It's a guinea pig!

9 **Look and match. Then circle.**

a What's the rabbit doing?
It's **running** / **swimming**.

b What's the lion doing?
It's **running** / **eating**.

c What's he doing?
He's **sleeping** / **eating**.

THINK BIG

Many families have animals. What are the most popular animals in your country?

7 Party Cakes

I will learn about cakes and desserts.

 1 **Listen, look, and say.**

 **1** chocolate cake	 **2** strawberry cake	 **3** fruitcake	 **4** gingerbread

 **5** ice cream cake	 **6** mooncakes	 **7** cupcakes

2 **Listen and check (✓).**

a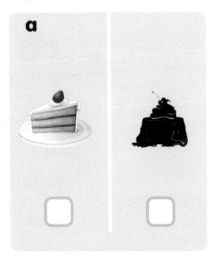

b

c

3 **Look, read and circle.**

a  He has **mooncakes / cupcakes.**

b I have an **gingerbread / ice cream cake.**

c They have a **chocolate cake / strawberry cake.**

4 **What cake do you like? Ask and answer with a partner. Draw.**

5 ▶ⓥ7 **Watch and stick in order. Then say.**

1	2	3	4

6 ▶ⓥ7 **Watch again. Match.**

a China

b India

c UK

d USA

designer bags

St. Paul's

smartphone

the Great Wall

the White House

Tower Bridge

7 🎧23 **Listen, read, and check (✓).**

a St. Paul's is a fruitcake.

b The Great Wall is a chocolate cake.

c The White House is gingerbread.

8 **Follow the lines. Ask and answer with a partner.**

What does she have?

She has a cupcake.

9 **Write. Then listen and check.** [24]

a What does he have? He has a chocolate cake.

b _____? They have two cupcakes.

c _____? She has three fruitcakes.

d _____? I have an ice cream cake.

What's the most popular cake in your class?
What's the least popular cake?

Flying Kites

 25

1 Listen, look, and say.

1 big

2 colorful

3 windy

4 beautiful

5 cool

6 successful

7 fun

8 high

26

2 Listen and circle. Then match.

a My kite is very big and **beautiful / high**.

b The kites are very **fun / high**.

c Flying kites is **beautiful / fun**.

(3) Listen, look, and say. ²⁷

 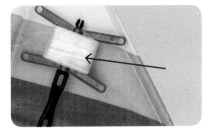 

plastic   string   sticks

4 Describe your perfect kite. Say with a partner. Draw.

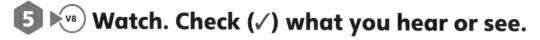

5 ▶ V8 **Watch. Check (✓) what you hear or see.**

☐ big ☐ beautiful ☐ windy ☐ high

6 ▶ V8 **Watch again. Match.**

a kite surfing   Guatemala

b kite festival   Egypt

c big kites   Thailand

28

7 **Listen, read, and circle.**

a Kite surfing is a popular **toy / sport**.

b The kites have **beautiful / windy** drawings.

c In Cairo, children are making their own **sticks / kites**.

8 **Follow the lines. Ask and answer with a partner.**

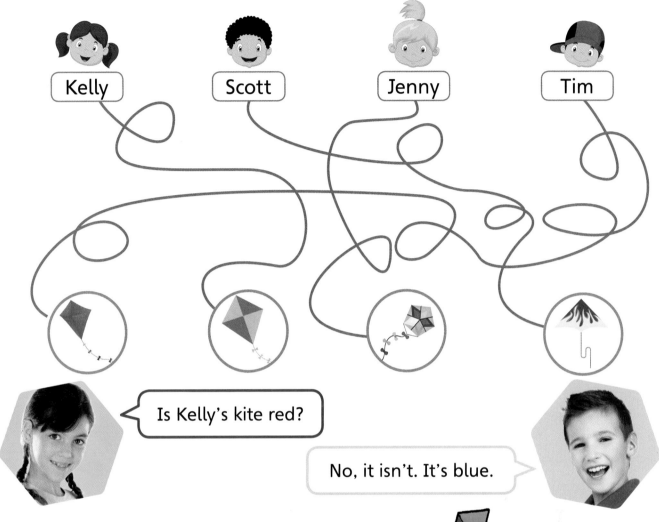

Kelly   Scott   Jenny   Tim

Is Kelly's kite red?

No, it isn't. It's blue.

9 **Read and color.**

Look at the children! They're flying their kites. It's a windy day.
Joe's kite is green and red. Alice's kite is yellow. They're beautiful!
Nathan's kite is orange, and Nina's kite is pink and purple. They're having so much fun!

Nathan

Alice   Nina

Joe

THINK BIG

What other toys fly? Make a list.

9 Let's Get Active

🎧 29 1 Listen, look, and say.

1 spin

2 kick

3 run

4 jump

5 flip

6 balance

7 practice tricks

8 dive

🎧 30 2 Listen and number.

a practice tricks

b jump

c run

d balance

(3) Listen, look, and say.

dance competition   parkour   skateboard

4 What actions can you do? Ask and answer with a partner. Draw.

5 ▶vq **Watch and stick in order. Then say.**

1	2	3

6 ▶vq **Watch again. Match.**

a parkour

b dancing

c skateboards

tricks

energetic

competition

7 🎧 **32 Listen, read, and check (✓).**

a A place in London is teaching parkour to children.

b Dancing is a fun play time activity.

c Some children in Ethiopia are playing with skateboards.

8 **Look. Ask and answer with a partner.**

Ted | RJ | Mary | Scott | Sam and Thomas

Is Ted running?

No, he isn't.
He's balancing.

9 **Read and match.**

a Is she spinning?

b Is he kicking?

c Are they jumping?

d Are they balancing?

No, he isn't. He's running.

Yes, they're jumping high!

Yes, she is.

No, they aren't.

THINK BIG

What are your classmates' favorite activities?
What don't they like to do?

Word List

1 School Time

by bicycle
by bus
by car
by taxi
by train
on foot
one
two
three
four

2 A New Family

baby
brother
cousins
family
father
friends
mother
sister

3 Use Your Body

hear
play
see
sign
smell
speak
taste
touch

ears
hands
head
mouth
nose

4 Clothes

cap
hat
kit
scarf
suit
tracksuit
T-shirt
horse race
soccer player
spectators
team manager

5 World Homes

apartment
chum
house
narrow boat
student home
tent
yurt
canal
solar panels
shipping containers
truck

6 Interesting Animals

bear
chicken
guinea pig
lamb
lion
pony
rabbit
sheep
tiger
elderly care home
farm
theme park

eat
run
sleep
swim

7 Party Cakes

chocolate cake
cupcakes
fruitcake
gingerbread
ice cream cake
mooncakes
strawberry cake

8 Flying Kites

beautiful
big
colorful
cool
fun
high
successful
windy
plastic
sticks
string

blue
green
orange
pink
purple
red
yellow

9 Let's Get Active

balance
dive
flip
jump
kick
practice tricks
run
spin
dance competition
parkour
skateboard